For Jena

Library of Congress Cataloging-in-Publication Data available.

ISBN: 978-0-8118-7723-7

Designed by Andy Rash

Typeset in Badhouse Bold and Corrosion. The artwork was painted in gouache on multipurpose paper and combined and colorized in Adobe Photoshop.

10 9 8 7 6 5 4 3 2

Chronicle Books LLC
680 Second Street
San Francisco, CA 94107
www.chroniclebooks.com

Ten little zombies

walking in a line

One stepped in a campfire

Now there are nine

Nine little zombies

climbing up a gate

One fell on a fence spear

Now there are eight

Eight little zombies

chasing after Kevin

Kevin shot his shotgun

Now there are seven

Seven little zombies
bursting through the bricks

One was crushed by statuary

Now there are six

Six little zombies
learning how to drive

Then they found the gas pedal

Now there are five

Five little zombies

scratching at my door

Acid through the transom

Now there are four

Four little zombies

coming after me

Fired up the chainsaw

Now there are three

Three little zombies

chasing after you

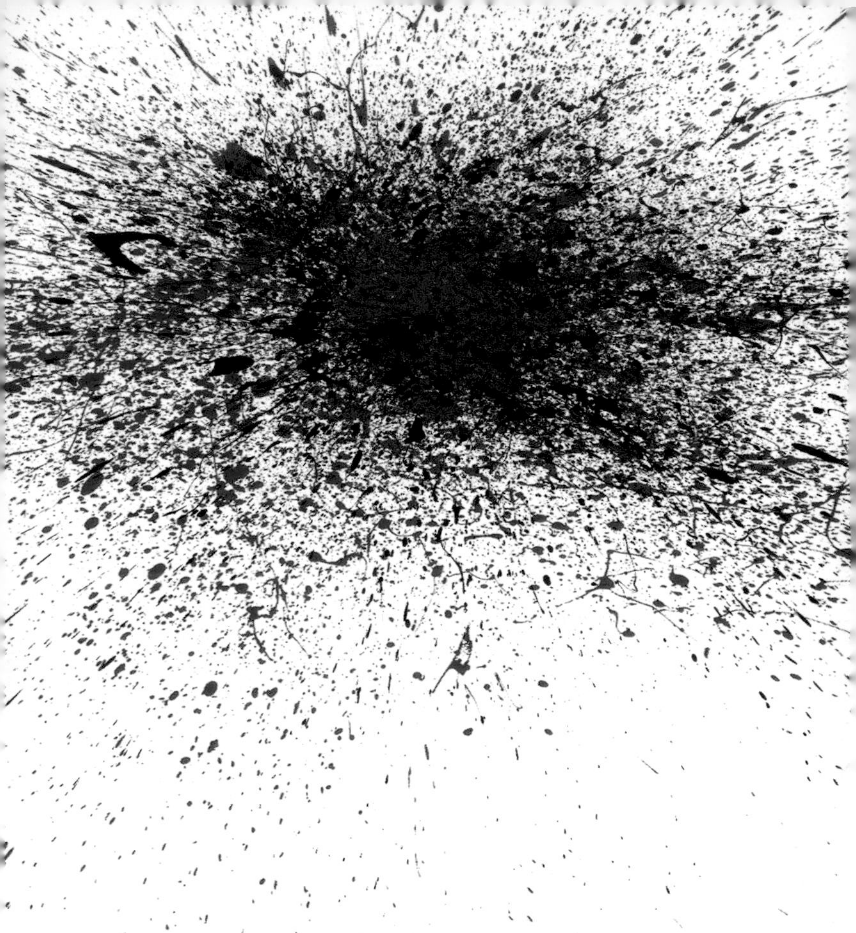

Sacrifice a hand grenade

Now there are two

Two little zombies

have us on the run

Empty out our nailguns

Now there is one

One little zombie

Tangled in the barbed wire

Now there are two

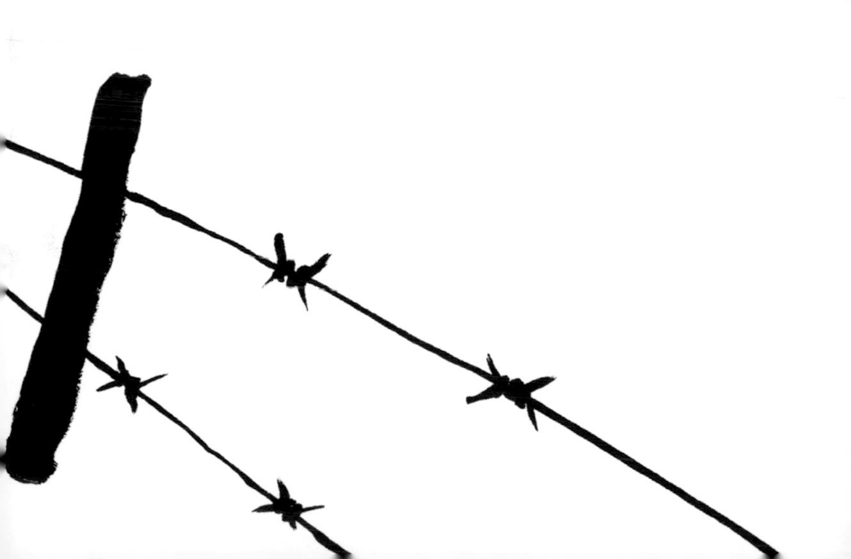

Two little zombies

coming
after
me

Can't bear to destroy you

Now there are...

BRAINS